QUICK GUIDE TO FINANCIAL SKILLS

QUICK GUIDE TO INSURANCE

by Kris Erickson Rowley

BrightPoint Press

San Diego, CA

BrightPoint Press

an imprint of ReferencePoint Press, Inc.
Printed in the United States

For more information, contact:
BrightPoint Press
PO Box 27779
San Diego, CA 92198
www.BrightPointPress.com

LIBRARY OF CONGRESS CATALOGING-IN-PUBLICATION DATA

Names: Rowley, Kris Erickson, author.
Title: Quick guide to insurance / by Kris Erickson Rowley.
Description: San Diego, CA: BrightPoint Press, [2025] | Series: Quick guide to financial skills | Includes bibliographical references and index. | Audience: Grades 7-9
Identifiers: LCCN 2024013364 (print) | LCCN 2024013365 (eBook) | ISBN 9781678209049 (hardcover) | ISBN 9781678209056 (eBook)
Subjects: LCSH: Insurance--Juvenile literature.
Classification: LCC HG8052.5.R69 2025 (print) | LCC HG8052.5 (eBook) | DDC 368--dc23/eng/20240405
LC record available at https://lccn.loc.gov/2024013364
LC eBook record available at https://lccn.loc.gov/2024013365

CONTENTS

AT A GLANCE

- Insurance protects people from financial loss caused by random events.
- People can buy insurance online or through an agent.
- Insurance companies sell policies. The policies cover certain events. If an event is covered, a policyholder can make a claim.
- Policyholders pay monthly premiums for their insurance policies. Premium prices are based on risk factors. For example, someone with a lot of speeding tickets might pay more for car insurance.
- A deductible is the amount of money a policyholder pays before insurance covers the rest.
- Property insurance pays to repair damage to homes and belongings when disaster strikes.

- Casualty insurance covers accidental damage. It also pays for the legal defense of a policyholder.
- Renters insurance covers a person's possessions, but not the building. Homeowners insurance covers possessions and the home itself.
- Health insurance helps pay medical bills.
- Life insurance gives a death payment to a beneficiary if the insured dies.
- Disability insurance pays a percentage of income to someone who is not able to return to work. Maternity leave can be covered under a disability policy. Illness or injury can also be covered.

HIT-AND-RUN

Sydney pulled out of the parking lot. She was a block from her apartment when she noticed a car to her left. It was about to run a stop sign. But it was too late for Sydney to brake. *Boom!* Sydney's car was hit hard. Shaking, she pulled over to check the damage. She expected the other car to pull over, too. But it sped away. Sydney couldn't make out the license plate number.

Staying calm after an accident helps people document all the information they need for insurance.

She looked around for witnesses. But she was alone.

Sydney's bumper was hanging off her car. She called her parents. Her dad said, "Thankfully you're not hurt. Your car can be fixed. Call the police. Then call your car insurance agent. The number is on the insurance card in your glove compartment. I'll call a tow truck."

Sydney called the police. An officer took the report over the phone. "There's not much we can do," the officer said. "There were no witnesses, and we don't have a plate number. But I'll send you the report."

Sydney called her insurance agent next. She told the agent what had happened.

The agent said, "Email me the police report. I'll file a claim for damages. This was

Many insurance companies allow people to file a claim online or through a mobile app.

a hit-and-run. The driver probably didn't have insurance. But you're covered for uninsured drivers. Is your car safe to drive?"

"I'm not sure," Sydney said. "But my dad called a tow truck."

"Tow it to a mechanic," the agent said. "They'll look at the damage. They'll estimate how much repairs will cost. Send me the estimate. Then we'll go from there."

The mechanic emailed Sydney that afternoon. The estimate was $3,563.57.

When a car can't be repaired, or fixing it will cost more than the car is worth, an insurance company totals the car.

Sydney forwarded the estimate and police report to her insurance agent. The agent submitted the claim of damages to Sydney's insurance company.

Later, the agent called Sydney to update her. "Normally, both drivers in an accident trade insurance information," her agent said. "The insurance companies work together to settle the claims. They figure out who was at fault. That person's insurance company pays for getting the cars fixed. But this was a hit-and-run. That means we don't have the other driver's insurance. Luckily, you have coverage for being hit by an uninsured driver. Your policy will pay for your repairs." Sydney was still upset about her car. But she was glad she had insurance!

Insurance helps keep bills from being too overwhelming after a disaster.

INSURANCE COVERAGE

Hundreds of years ago, people formed groups to help each other recover from bad events. Insurance companies came from this idea. Car accidents like Sydney's are common. Fires and storms cause losses and harm. People also get sick or injured. In these emergencies, insurance can help.

Insurance companies insure random events that cause damage. If damage is covered in a policy, the insurance company pays the **policyholder**. Insurance agent and author Bart Baker says, "Insurance is a way to help put your life back in order."[1]

WHAT IS INSURANCE?

Some people don't want to pay for something they might not need. But budgeting expert Tiffany Aliche explains why insurance is useful. "If you don't have it when you need it, you can get yourself into some big trouble," she says. "Insurance is a risk management tool. The reason you get insurance is to protect you in case something happens."[2] Disasters can wipe out savings. Insurance protects from

On August 10, 2020, the most expensive thunderstorm in history ripped through the midwestern United States. Insurance companies paid billions of dollars to fix damages.

financial loss. But it must be purchased *before* disaster strikes. The Grange Insurance website says, "The most difficult thing about insurance is that you're paying for something you hope you never have to use. Nobody wants something bad

People can buy insurance to cover travel, events, weddings, and more.

to happen to them. But suffering a loss without insurance can put you in a difficult financial situation."[3]

TYPES OF INSURANCE

Three types of insurance are important for young adults. These are car, health, and renters or homeowners insurance. Almost all states require **liability** car insurance. This covers property damage and injuries to people. Health insurance covers injuries and illness. Renters insurance covers belongings that are damaged or stolen. Homeowners insurance covers belongings and the home itself.

Life and **disability** insurance should also be considered. Life insurance pays a lump sum when the insured person dies.

Disability insurance pays when disability or illness keeps a person from working. These types of insurance can be important for a family under stress.

UNDERSTANDING INSURANCE TERMS

An insurance policy is an agreement between an insurance company and a policyholder. The company agrees to pay the policyholder if losses occur. The losses must be listed in the policy to be covered.

The insured pays a monthly premium for the policy. Policy prices vary. The more the plan covers, the higher the premium. Policy price is also affected by risk factors. For example, someone who smokes might pay more for life insurance.

An insurance claim is a request sent to an insurance company. The claim tells the company that a loss happened. It asks the insurance company to pay for the damages. Then the company checks whether the losses are covered. If the claim is approved, the insured gets paid.

A deductible is how much a policyholder pays to repair damages. The insurance

First American Insurance Company

In 1752, Benjamin Franklin helped found the first American insurance company. It was called the Philadelphia Contributionship. It insured houses from loss by fire. Policyholders bought 7-year fire policies. The company eventually expanded. It still exists today.

An insurance policy lists the terms, including the premium price, deductible, and what the policy covers.

company pays for the rest of the damages. A person's deductible amount is stated in the policy.

HOW TO BUY INSURANCE

Insurance companies sell policies in many ways. People can select policies themselves online. They can also buy through insurance agents. Agents are licensed professionals. They have lots of knowledge about insurance.

Some agents represent many companies. They are known as independent insurance agents. These agents have a wide selection of policies to offer. Other agents work with a single company or group. They are known as captive agents. Agents provide services

Insurance agents help customers find the best policy for their needs.

to their customers. They help people make sure they have enough coverage for their **assets**. Agents help out when damage occurs.

People can shop around to find the best insurance for their budget. A price estimate is called a quote. The Missouri Department of Insurance suggests getting at least three quotes before making a decision.

"With Internet shopping, three quotes take no time at all," it advises. "You could probably get 20 quotes in the same amount of time it takes to drive to or call three agents. The more you shop, the better price you will find."[4]

Buying insurance can feel overwhelming. But there are many resources available to help. People should do research before choosing a policy. This will help them find the best fit for their needs.

CHAPTER TWO

PROPERTY AND CASUALTY INSURANCE

Property insurance covers possessions. **Casualty** insurance covers damages. It also covers risks from lawsuits. Property and casualty insurance are usually sold together as a package. Car and homeowners insurance are examples.

Property insurance protects homes, cars, and more from **perils**. Fire is considered a peril. Other perils include damage from hail, wind, power surges, and heavy snow.

Most homeowners insurance policies do not cover floods. People in areas where floods are common must buy separate flood insurance.

SUZUKI
BLUE RIDGE

Insurance policies say which perils are covered. Something not listed in the policy is likely not insured. They also explain how much can be paid. Insurance should have enough coverage to replace belongings and buildings. Underinsuring can lead to losses.

Casualty insurance protects policyholders from lawsuits. It covers the cost of legal defense and payment for damages. For example, a homeowner's deck could collapse. Those injured could sue the homeowner. Casualty insurance would cover medical bills for those injured. It would pay for the homeowner's legal defense.

RENTERS AND HOME INSURANCE

Renters insurance covers loss or damage to everything inside a rented space. It includes liability coverage if someone is injured. But it doesn't include the building. The landlord's insurance covers that. For example, Layna lives in an apartment building. Her upstairs neighbor lets the tub overflow. Water comes through Layna's ceiling. It damages

People can buy extra coverage for expensive items such as instruments, electronics, and jewelry.

her couch and laptop. Layna's insurance covers her belongings. It pays her to buy replacements. The landlord's insurance pays to fix the ceiling.

Homeowners insurance covers damage to the home itself. A roof could be damaged by hail. Insurance would pay for repairs. It also covers things inside the house, such as furniture and clothing. Homeowner's insurance also includes casualty coverage.

Theft

Renters and homeowners insurance help replace a person's stolen possessions. This includes break-ins. But it can also include thefts that happen away from home. A laptop might be stolen from a car. Luggage could be stolen on vacation. Many policies would cover these thefts. They may cover less than in-home thefts.

AUTO INSURANCE

Almost every state requires liability insurance on vehicles. This covers damage caused to other cars or property in an accident. It also covers any injuries the insured causes. It does not cover the insured's own injuries. It also doesn't cover damages to the insured's car.

Other types of car insurance give full coverage. Collision insurance covers damage from road hazards or other cars. Comprehensive insurance covers damage caused by animals. It also covers natural disasters, theft, and vandalism.

There are also add-ons to full coverage. Medical payments coverage (MedPay) is one. Personal injury protection (PIP) is another. MedPay covers some medical expenses for people in car accidents. This includes if they are at fault for the accident. It also can cover passengers. PIP pays medical expenses for the insured and passengers. It also pays for lost wages if a person misses work due to injuries. MedPay or PIP are required in some states.

Uninsured and underinsured motorist coverage are other add-ons. They are usually sold together. Some states require them. People might drive without liability insurance. They could cause an accident. Their victims would have to pay for their own injuries and damages. Uninsured motorist coverage helps cover these costs. Underinsured motorist coverage is similar. The at-fault driver's insurance might not fully

Car insurance does not cover basic maintenance or wear and tear.

Car theft is covered under comprehensive insurance. This insurance doesn't cover theft of items inside a car, but renters or homeowners insurance might.

pay for damages. Underinsured coverage helps cover the difference.

Companies set a policy's price based on the risk of a driver causing damages. The more likely the risk, the more likely prices will go up. Past accidents and speeding tickets are considered. So are the type of car and the age of the driver. Bart Baker says, "Young drivers are expensive to insure—and rightfully so. The number of claims filed by this group of drivers is dramatically more than that of experienced drivers."[5]

Insurance companies review claims each year. They may increase the premium. They may not renew customers considered too risky. They also may not renew customers who submit too many claims. For these reasons, it's sometimes better to pay for smaller damages out-of-pocket.

WAYS TO CUT COSTS

There are ways to lower premium prices. Many companies give discounts to students with good grades. People with two or more insurance policies at the same company often get discounts. This is called bundling. Cars with safety equipment may also get discounts. So might those with anti-theft equipment. But these cars are more expensive to fix. This means the insurance will likely be more expensive. It often costs more to insure new cars than used cars. Rates depend on the car's make and model.

Many companies give discounts for safe driving. This can be based on having no reported accidents or tickets. It can also be based on telematics, or usage-based insurance. These programs actively track drivers. This is often done through a smartphone app or a device in the car. Safe driving is rewarded.

Teen drivers are expensive to insure, but good grades can help.

A higher deductible lowers the premium. But this raises out-of-pocket expenses. People may also be able to lower costs by shopping around with different companies.

Property and casualty insurance may seem expensive. But they provide valuable protection. Insurance helps people have peace of mind.

CHAPTER THREE

HEALTH INSURANCE

Health insurance helps pay for medical treatment. It reduces the cost of accidents or illness. It also pays for yearly physicals, maternity care, and some prescriptions.

Health insurance policies are written to cover a policyholder for one year. The policy is paid each month. The cost depends on what the plan includes. The more services it covers, the higher the price.

Health insurance helps cover medical costs.

HEALTH INSURANCE PLANS

There are several types of health insurance in the United States. Some are government insurance plans for low-income and disabled people. These include Medicaid and the Children's Health Insurance Program (CHIP). Medicare covers people 65 or older.

Some insurance plans have a network of providers. Patients must use the providers in the network. Insurance may not cover the full cost if patients use other providers.

Flexible spending accounts (FSAs) are not insurance. But they go along with it. FSAs let people save money for medical expenses. Money is taken from a person's paycheck. The money goes into a flexible spending account. It can be used to pay

People can use FSA and HSA funds to buy cough medicine, bandages, and other nonprescription medical needs.

for costs not covered by insurance. These include deductibles and copays. FSA funds can also be used for over-the-counter medications or first aid items. Any money put in the account must be spent that year.

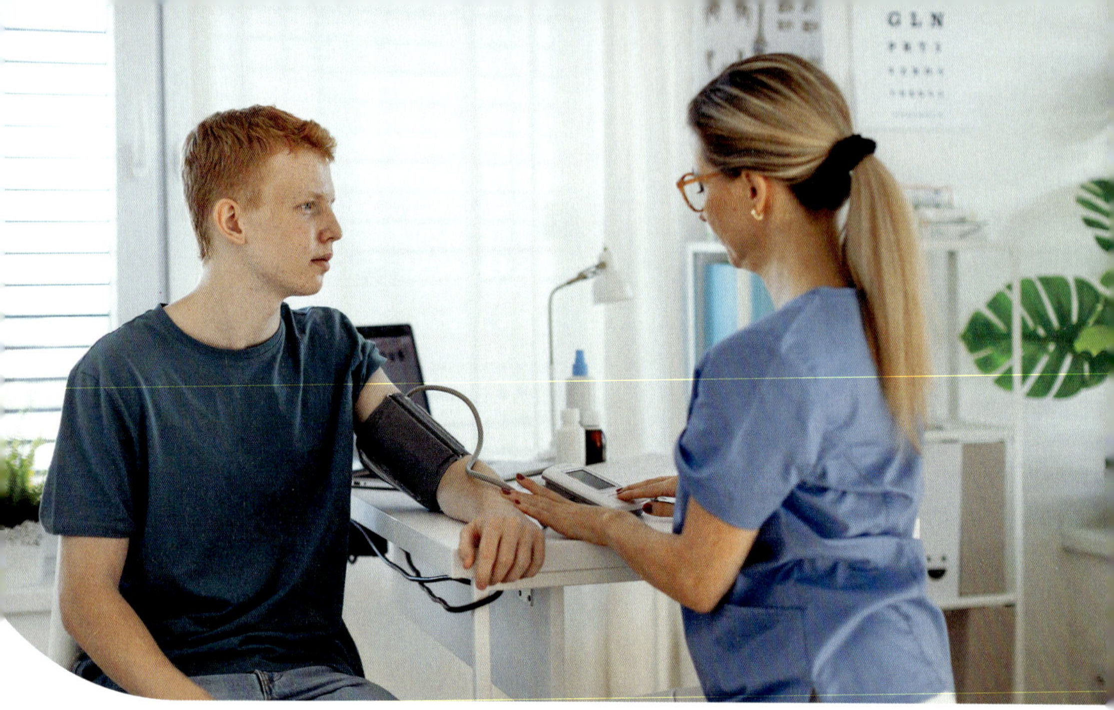

Insurance usually fully covers services such as yearly physicals. Patients may need to pay for other care.

Health savings accounts (HSAs) are similar. But they are only for people with high-deductible insurance. In 2024, plans with at least a $1,600 deductible qualified as high deductible. HSA balances can carry over from year to year.

HOW HEALTH INSURANCE PAYS

Sometimes health insurance pays the full amount for care. This is common for wellness services such as annual physicals. Most of the time, costs are shared between the company and policyholder. This is called coinsurance. The policyholder pays the deductible. Then he pays a percentage of the bill. Insurance pays the rest. The deductible might be $250. The insured pays 20 percent of the remaining amount. Insurance pays the other 80 percent.

Policies also have flat fees. These are called copayments, or copays. The policyholder pays a copay for some services. Copays are usually $25 or less. But they can vary.

Corey is 21 years old. He is covered by his mother's health insurance policy. The policy has a $250 deductible. Corey broke his arm. The bill cost $1,500.

Corey paid the $250 deductible. That left $1,250. Corey paid $250 more. This was his 20 percent coinsurance. His insurance paid $1,000. This was insurance's 80 percent coinsurance.

There are limits to how much someone pays out of pocket for medical bills each

Supplemental Health Insurance

Supplemental insurance plans add extra coverage. They are not meant to replace health insurance. Dental and vision insurance are usually considered supplemental. Supplemental insurance can also cover accidents or hospital stays. It can give coverage if a person is diagnosed with specific diseases. Money from supplemental insurance can often be used to cover nonmedical expenses. These include groceries, childcare, and more.

year. A policyholder may hit the limit. Then insurance will pay all her remaining medical bills for that year. In 2024, the maximum limit was $9,450 for individuals. It was $18,900 for families.

PURCHASING INSURANCE

Many people in the United States get health insurance through work. The employer pays part of the monthly premium. The employee pays the rest. Some people buy insurance plans on their own. They pay the entire price.

People can buy insurance on the HealthCare.gov website. This is a national health insurance database. HealthCare.gov was set up in 2010. It was part of a law called the Affordable Care

Act (ACA). This law created protections for people with preexisting health conditions. Insurance providers can no longer deny policies to people with these conditions. The ACA also allowed most children to stay on their parents' health insurance until age 26.

US healthcare is expensive. Health insurance can help lighten the load. People benefit from understanding their policy and knowing what it covers.

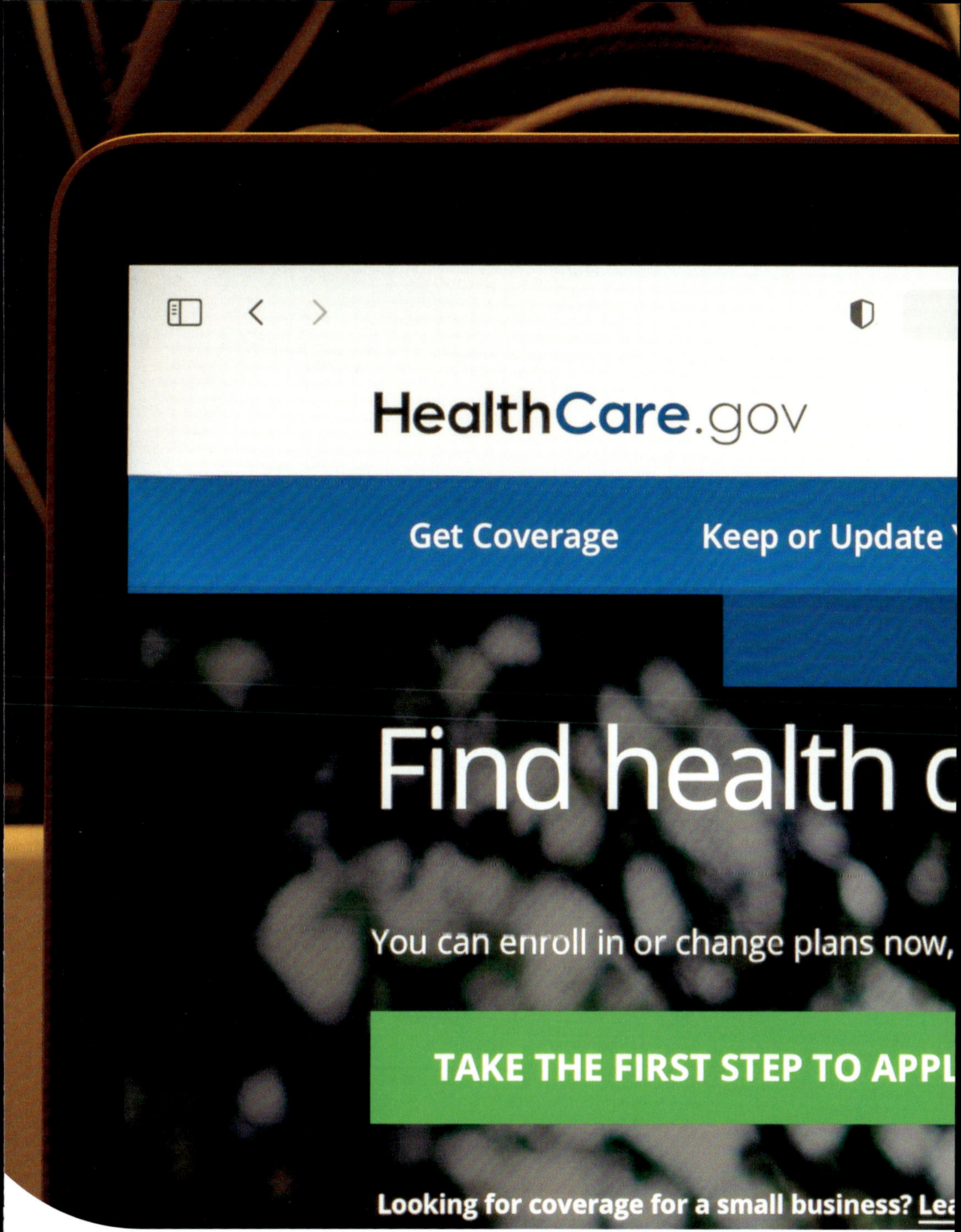

HealthCare.gov is home to a national health insurance database as well as informative articles about health insurance.

CHAPTER FOUR

LIFE AND DISABILITY INSURANCE

When a loved one dies, the surviving family faces many challenges. One may be the loss of income. Life insurance can't bring a loved one back. But it can pay a death benefit. This can help support the family.

Life insurance is a formal contract. The insured chooses **beneficiaries**. If the policyholder dies, the beneficiaries are paid.

People with family who depend on their income should consider life insurance.

Opening a life insurance policy as a young adult can lock in lower premium rates.

Payments on the policy must be up to date to receive a benefit.

Young adults may not need life insurance. But there are situations in which they should consider it. Life insurance can protect spouses and children after an insured's death. It can also pay off large debts. "Think of your life insurance policy as a bridge. It's there to protect you and your family as you're building wealth," Tiffany Aliche says.[6]

BUYING A POLICY

Life insurance companies look at age and health when setting prices. The older someone is, the higher the risk of death. And the higher the risk, the higher the price. Life insurance usually costs less for young adults. Many policies lock in the starting rate. A 20-year-old can start a policy. She will pay the same rate throughout the term. This is a benefit to starting young.

A person must apply to buy life insurance. She provides her medical history. She lists any preexisting medical conditions. Accidents and speeding tickets are also considered. Applicants must list risky hobbies, such as car racing. A medical exam may be required. The insurance company uses this information to set the policy price. It also **guarantees** the death benefit amount.

People should review their policies every year. Beneficiaries may need to be changed. Health risks listed in the policy should also be reviewed. People can purchase additional coverage, called riders. Riders can cover accidents, illnesses,

Pet Insurance

Many people consider their pets to be family. But veterinary care is not covered by regular insurance. Pet owners may buy pet insurance. Some policies cover only accidents. Eating something dangerous would be an accident. Others cover illnesses, too. People can add on extra coverage for routine care. Prices vary based on coverage and deductibles. A pet's age and breed also play a role in cost.

and more. Any policy updates must be signed and dated before they go into effect.

TEMPORARY AND PERMANENT LIFE INSURANCE

There are two types of life insurance policies. Temporary life insurance is active for a fixed number of years. Permanent life insurance lasts until the insured dies.

Temporary insurance is known as term life insurance. This is the most common type. It is usually less expensive. The premium is paid each month until the policy expires. It usually covers a person's working years. By retirement age, some people don't need life insurance anymore. They have paid off debt. Their children have grown. They have money from other assets.

Term life is a good option for these people. Some people might not want to pay for a policy that may not pay out. Aliche says,

> *Life insurance is a risk management tool, just like car insurance. If you pay for your car insurance . . . and you never use it, are you going to be mad that you never got into an accident so you could have used your insurance? I don't think so.*[7]

People should compare the costs and the benefits of different policies.

Whole life and universal life are permanent life insurance policies. These policies are more expensive. Premiums are paid monthly until death. Beneficiaries receive the promised sum after the insured's death. The insured can borrow against a

Term life insurance policies don't cover a person's whole life. But they are much less expensive than permanent policies.

permanent policy while alive. Permanent policies may be good options for people with family members who are unable to work. The policy can offer support after the insured's death.

Group life insurance is often available through a person's job. An employer usually pays all or some of the premium. This can be an affordable insurance option. There are usually no coverage limits. This means anyone can be covered, even people with health issues. But the policy may expire if a person leaves his job. Benefits are usually lower than with individual policies.

DISABILITY INSURANCE

Disability insurance helps when a person can't work. It pays a percentage of the person's income. The policy must be in place before the disability occurs. Insurance is sold by how long the disability is expected to last. Short-term disability gives benefits for a limited time. This might be a few weeks or months. Policies cover temporary conditions that keep a person

Disability insurance helps people who can't work due to an injury or disability.

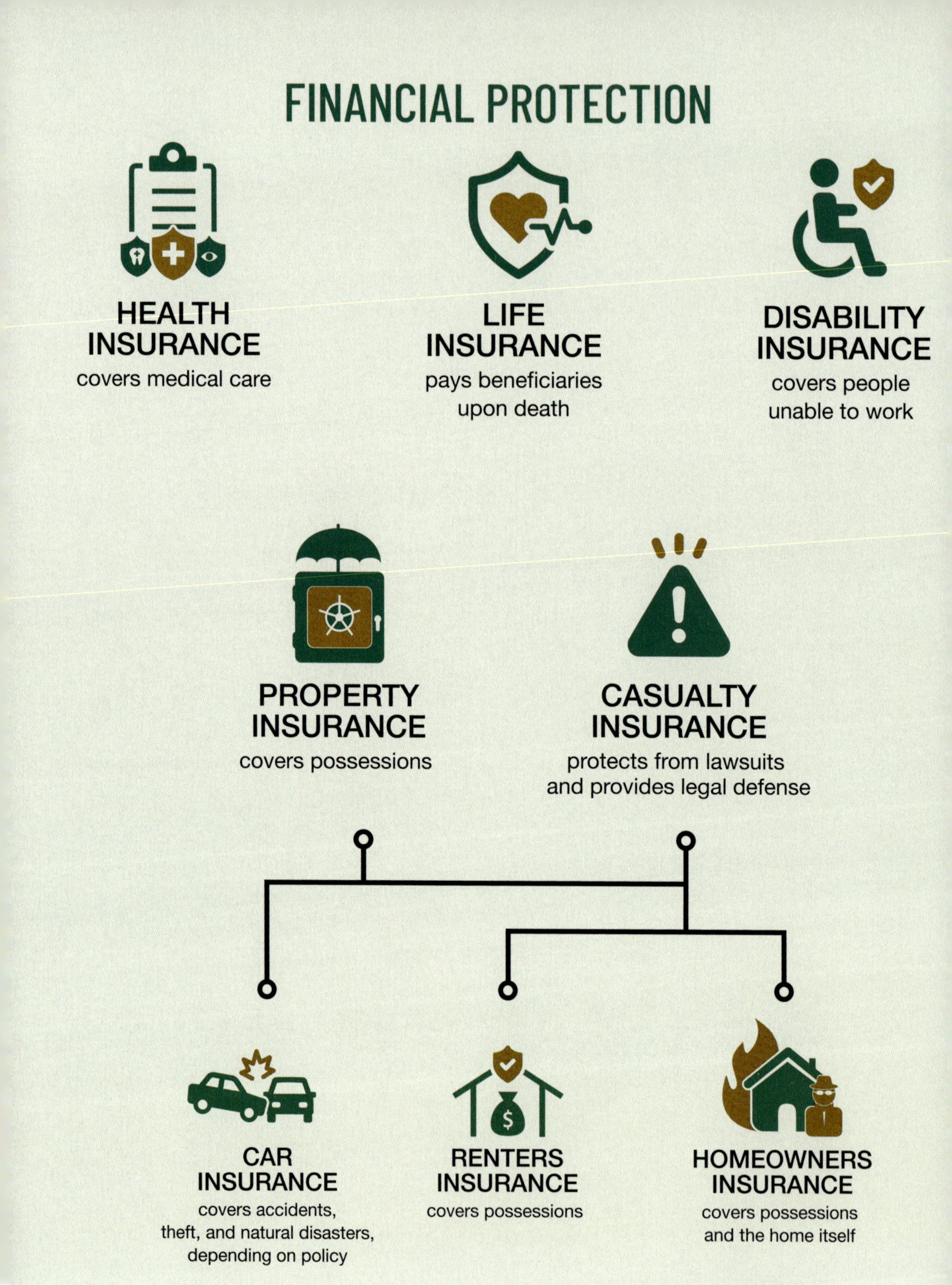

Insurance offers financial protection from disasters.

from working. Long-term disability insurance can last for several years. It covers more serious disabilities.

THE BIG PICTURE

Insurance isn't something people can see. But it gives real protection to a person's assets. An insurance policy locks in financial help when bad things happen. Jessica Wei writes for the money app MyDoh. She says,

> *Mostly, insurance pays for peace of mind. When an emergency happens, the last thing anyone wants or needs is a financial burden on top of an emotional one. . . . Paying out a modest monthly premium could be easier than absorbing the full brunt of an unfortunate incident.*[8]

GLOSSARY

assets

things that make up a person's wealth, such as money or property

beneficiaries

people designated on an insurance policy to obtain money after a death

casualty

an accident, mishap, or disaster

disability

a physical or mental condition that limits a person's ability to do certain tasks

guarantees

provides a promise that something will be fulfilled after certain conditions occur

liability

responsibility for something, such as paying for damages

perils

unpredictable events that cause damage

policyholder

the person who owns an insurance policy

SOURCE NOTES

INTRODUCTION: HIT-AND-RUN

1. Bart Baker, *If an Elephant Sits on You, Are You Covered? How to Talk to Your Insurance Agent to be Properly Insured*. Malibu, CA: Think It Publishing, 2014, p. 17.

CHAPTER ONE: WHAT IS INSURANCE?

2. Tiffany Aliche, *Get Good with Money*. New York: Harmony Books, 2021, p. 236.

3. "What Is Insurance and Why Is It Important?" *Grange Insurance*, n.d. www.grangeinsurance.com.

4. "Don't Risk It," *Missouri Department of Insurance*, n.d. http://insurance.mo.gov.

CHAPTER TWO: PROPERTY AND CASUALTY INSURANCE

5. Baker, *If an Elephant Sits on You, Are You Covered?* p. 45.

CHAPTER FOUR: LIFE AND DISABILITY INSURANCE

6. Aliche, *Get Good with Money*, p. 254.

7. Aliche, *Get Good with Money*, pp. 246–247.

8. Jessica Wei, "Insurance 101: A Guide for Parents and Teens," *MyDoh*, March 25, 2022. www.mydoh.ca.

FOR FURTHER RESEARCH

BOOKS

Sue Bradford Edwards, *Tornadoes*. San Diego, CA: BrightPoint Press, 2025.

Carol Hand, *What You Need to Know about Health Insurance*. New York: Rosen, 2020.

Marne Ventura, *Quick Guide to Renting*. San Diego, CA: BrightPoint Press, 2025.

INTERNET SOURCES

"How Insurance Works," *Invest*, n.d. www.investprogram.org.

"Understanding and Navigating Your Insurance Policy," *UF Health*, n.d. http://shcc.ufl.edu/fees-and-insurance.

"Understanding Renter's Insurance," *South Carolina Department of Insurance*, January 6, 2023. www.doi.sc.gov.

WEBSITES

HealthCare.gov
www.healthcare.gov

HealthCare.gov is the US national health insurance database. People can find and purchase health insurance on this website. The site also provides general information about health insurance in the United States.

NerdWallet
www.nerdwallet.com

The NerdWallet website provides information and guides on various financial topics, including insurance.

Progressive Answers
www.progressive.com/answers

Progressive is a US insurance provider. Its Answers site provides informative articles on various types of insurance.

INDEX

IMAGE CREDITS

Cover: © Monkey Business Images/Shutterstock Images
5: © thodonal88/Shutterstock Images
7: © hedgehog94/Shutterstock Images
9: © Kaspars Grinvalds/Shutterstock Images
10: © SKT Studio/Shutterstock Images
12: © fizkes/Shutterstock Images
15: © Darrell Werning/National Weather Service/NOAA
16: © RedPixel.PL/Shutterstock Images
20: © nito/Shutterstock Images
22: © BalanceFormCreative/Shutterstock Images
25: © Jon Rehg/Shutterstock Images
27: © PattyPhoto/Shutterstock Images
31: © Pixel-Shot/Shutterstock Images
32: © Gina Buliga/Shutterstock Images
35: © Motortion Films/Shutterstock Images
37: © DC Studio/Shutterstock Images
39: © BearFotos/Shutterstock Images
40: © Halfpoint/Shutterstock Images
45: © Tada Images/Shutterstock Images
47: © Chompoo Suriyo/Shutterstock Images
48: © fizkes/Shutterstock Images
53: © Ground Picture/Shutterstock Images
55: © Antonio Guillem/Shutterstock Images
56 (health, life, disability, casualty, car, renters [house]): © The Studio/Shutterstock Images
56 (property, renters [bag of money], homeowners): © SoleilC/Shutterstock Images

ABOUT THE AUTHOR

Kris Erickson Rowley is mother to four grown children. Her hobbies are running trails, storytelling, and freelance writing. She has served as elected County Treasurer since 2007 and on the Iowa Public Employees' Retirement System's Investment Board since 2020. She lives with her husband in Spirit Lake, Iowa.